DAD'S PICKLEBALL JOKES

By Richard Eklund

Copyright© 2024 Rip N LV LLC, dba Bear Naked Pickleball.

BearNakedPickleball.com

All rights reserved. Printed and bound in the United States of America.

No part of this book may be used or reproduced in any manner whatsoever without written permission except in the case of brief quotations embodied in critical articles and reviews.

Dad's Pickleball Jokes / by Richard Eklund

Summary: An illustrated collection of jokes related to Pickleball.

ISBN 979-8-218-53395-3

Dad's Pickleball Jokes

Dedication

I want to dedicate this book to Savannah and Sierra who have listened to my 'bad' dad jokes for a lifetime.

To my mom who taught me to laugh.

To Carolyn who listens to all my jokes, in and out of this book, and who continues to inspire me everyday.

To Todd and Ylldes who have always believed in me and encouraged me.

And of course, to all my friends on the Pickleball court. I am grateful for all the fun times we have spent together.

Dad's Pickleball Jokes

Dr... I Presume

Why is Frankenstein good at Pickleball?

😆 Because he's a MONSTER on the court!

Dad's Pickleball Jokes

Youngsters on the Court

What do you call a young girl who plays Pickleball?

 A Cute-cumber

Dad's Pickleball Jokes

Wow Dude!

Why didn't the man with the expensive sports car play Pickleball?

 Because he was having a MID-COURT Crisis!

Dad's Pickleball Jokes

Relish Tray

Why was the olive jealous of the pickle?

 Because he didn't have a sport named after him!

Dad's Pickleball Jokes

Ladies of the Court

What do you call a lady in the middle of the Pickleball Court?

 ANNETTE

Dad's Pickleball Jokes

Page 7

Who's?

What's the last thing you hear as the ball goes down the middle between you and your partner?

 YOURS!

Dad's Pickleball Jokes

From the Barber Shop

Why do people like to play Pickleball with barbers?

 Because they have **STYLE**

Dad's Pickleball Jokes

Blue Light Special

What do you call it when the score is: 2 - 4 - 1?

 BOGO

Dad's Pickleball Jokes

It's Getting Hot in Here

Why aren't Chefs good at Pickleball?

 Because they are always standing in the Kitchen!

Dad's Pickleball Jokes

Yummm!

What do Pickleball players eat after dinner?

 A DILLicious dessert!

Dad's Pickleball Jokes — Page 12

Monster Math

Why was 2 afraid of 7?

 Because 7-8-1 (seven ate one)!

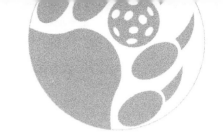

Dad's Pickleball Jokes — Page 13

Bunny Time!

Why was the Easter Bunny picking up all the Pickleballs?

 Because he thought they were HOLY EGGS!

Dad's Pickleball Jokes — Page 14

Winners on the Court

What do you call the Pickleball Tournament Champions?

 Big DILLs

Dad's Pickleball Jokes

Hey Bartender!

Why are Bartenders good at Pickleball?

 Because they make SHOTS!

Dad's Pickleball Jokes

Page 16

Whoa.... from the Underworld

Why doesn't the Devil play Pickleball?

 Because the balls are HOLY!

Dad's Pickleball Jokes

Pickleball Pirates

Why don't people like to play Pickleball with Pirates?

 Because they ARRRGUE too much.

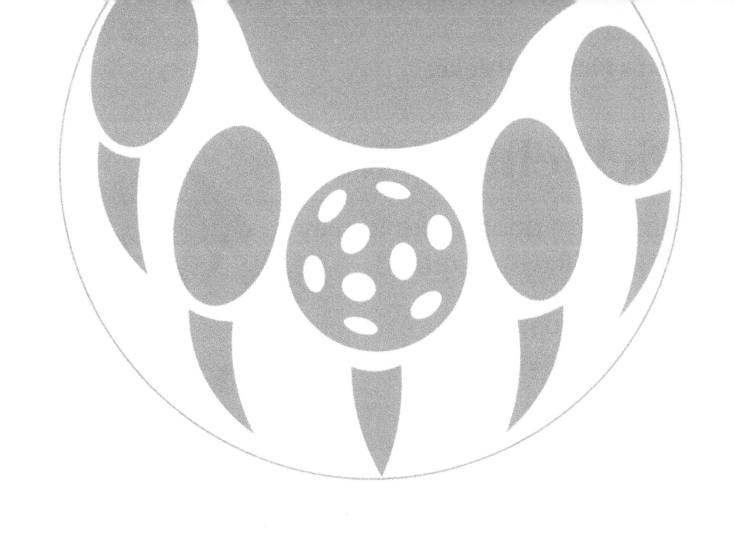

Dad's Pickleball Jokes   Page 18

Seafood Delight

What do you call a bad LOB that gets smashed back?

 LOBster dinner

Dad's Pickleball Jokes

Over Served

What do you call a Pickleball player that Dinks too much?

 A Dunk!

Dad's Pickleball Jokes — Page 20

Knight Me!

What title do you bestow upon a Pickleball Player that likes to dink all the time?

 Sir Dink-A-Lot!

Dad's Pickleball Jokes

$$$$$

Why don't people like to be Pickleball partners with Stock Brokers?

 Because they're all TRADERS!

Dad's Pickleball Jokes

Farm Fresh

Why didn't anyone want to play Pickleball with the Pig?

 Because he was a ball HOG

Dad's Pickleball Jokes

Rules and Rulers!

What do you call a Pickleball net that is too high?

 Regulation!

Dad's Pickleball Jokes

Page 24

Give me an Order!

What do you call a score of 1-1-1?

 French Fries

BONUS: What do you call a score of 11-11-1?

 Supersized Fries

Dad's Pickleball Jokes

Clandestine Activities

What do you call a Pickleball Spy?

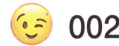 002

Dad's Pickleball Jokes

Anchors Aweigh!

Why aren't Sailors good at Pickleball?

 Because they don't know how to use PADDLES

Dad's Pickleball Jokes

Count Pickula

Why do people like to play Pickleball with Count Dracula?

 Because he's good at COUNTING the score

Dad's Pickleball Jokes

Can I take your order?

Why are Waitresses good at Pickleball?

 Because they are good SERVERS

Dad's Pickleball Jokes Page 29

Let's all Play!

What do you call an assortment of Pickleball players?

😃 DILLversity

Dad's Pickleball Jokes

Jurassic Court

Why couldn't the T-Rex play Pickleball two days in a row?

 Because he was Dino-Sore!

Dad's Pickleball Jokes

Can You Tell Me How to Get...?

What do Pickleball and Sesame Street have in common?

 They both have a Bert and an Erne!

Dad's Pickleball Jokes

Order UP!

Why was the fast food cook so good at Pickleball?

 Because he could really move around the kitchen!

Dad's Pickleball Jokes Page 33

Good Times

What do you call a long day of playing Pickleball?

 A Great day

Dad's Pickleball Jokes

Shizzalicious

What is the Rapper's favorite Pickleball shot?

😎   Drop it …
     like it's HOT!

Dad's Pickleball Jokes

Show me the Bling

What's a Pickleball players favorite jewelry?

 DILLver

Dad's Pickleball Jokes

What will you have?

What did the Waiter say after he won the point?

 You've been SERVED!

Dad's Pickleball Jokes

Okay Officer

What did the Policeman tell the Pickleball players?

 Dink Responsibly!

Dad's Pickleball Jokes

Down the River

Why are Kayakers good at Pickleball?

🙂 Because they know how to use paddles!

Dad's Pickleball Jokes Page 39

Can I Have a Piece?

What was the Pizza Chef's favorite Pickleball shot?

 The SLICE!

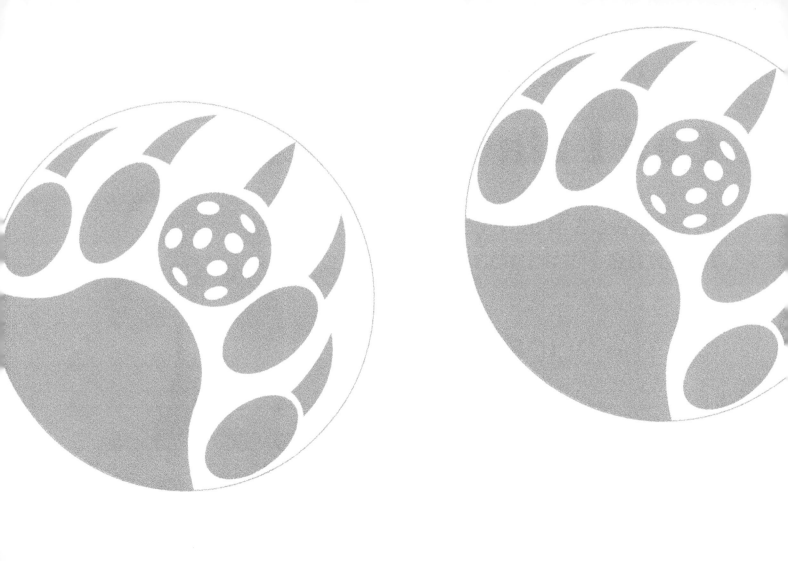

Dad's Pickleball Jokes

Out to Sea

Why wasn't the fish very good at Pickleball?

 Because he kept getting caught in the NET!

Dad's Pickleball Jokes

Haunted House

What is the scariest room in the house for Pickleball players?

 The Kitchen!

Dad's Pickleball Jokes

Race Car Legend

Why is Ricky Bobby (the race car driver) good at Pickleball?

 Because he's a professional at the SHAKE and BAKE!

Dad's Pickleball Jokes

Cindy in the House!

What kind of dance does a Pickleball player go to?

 A PickleBALL!

Dad's Pickleball Jokes

Page 44

Eww

What did the Pickleball referee say to the Skunk who was cheating?

 Odor on the Court!

Dad's Pickleball Jokes

Pan Me

What do you call a fairy that plays Pickleball?

🤣 DinkerBell

Dad's Pickleball Jokes — Page 46

Bearly There?

Why wasn't the Koala Bear allowed in the Pickleball tournament?

 Because he wasn't Koala-fied!

Dad's Pickleball Jokes

Page 47

Cloudy with a chance of...!

What do you call it when the weather is great for playing Pickleball?

 DILLightful!

Dad's Pickleball Jokes

Station 11

Why was the Fireman good at Pickleball?

 Because he was skilled at putting out fires in the Kitchen!

Dad's Pickleball Jokes

Where's my Package?

What job did the Pickleball player do when he wasn't playing Pickleball?

 He was a DILLivery driver!

Dad's Pickleball Jokes

Over the Barrel !

Why didn't the cucumber want to play Pickleball?

 He didn't want to get PICKLED!

Dad's Pickleball Jokes

Do it Your Way!

What did the King Burger say to his opponents?

   Hold the PICKLE!

Dad's Pickleball Jokes

Page 52

Where Did That Come From?

What do you call a Bad Lob?

 BLOB!

Dad's Pickleball Jokes　　　　　　　　　　　　　　　　　　Page 53

Can We Play?

Knock knock!
　Who's there?
Pickleball!
　Pickleball who?
 Pick-a-ball and let's play!

Dad's Pickleball Jokes

Nacho Cheese!

Why did the mouse keep stealing the pickleballs?

 Because he thought they were CHEESEBALLS!

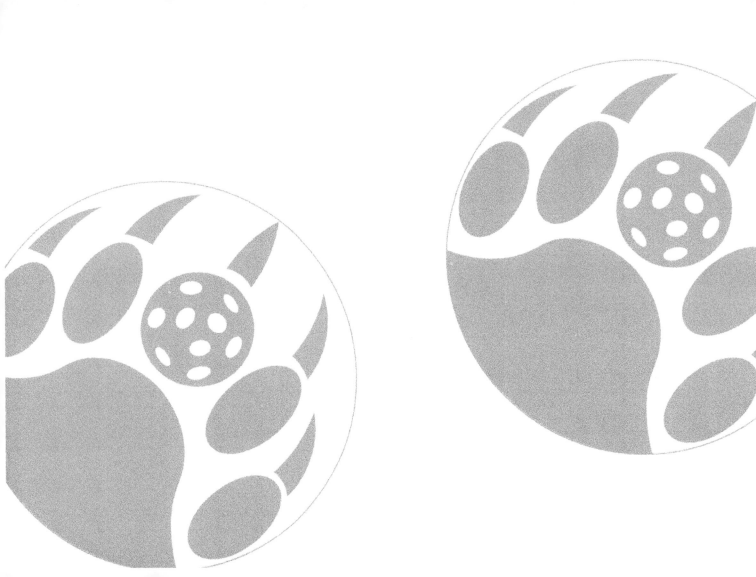

Dad's Pickleball Jokes — Page 55

Tip the Man!

What did the Pickleball Player want for dinner after the match?

😉 A DILLuxe Pizza DILLivered!

Dad's Pickleball Jokes   Page 56

Walking...!

What is the Zombie's favorite Pickleball shot?

 The BODY BAG!

Dad's Pickleball Jokes — Page 57

Slow is Fast!

Why was the sloth hard to beat in Pickleball?

😉 Because he just kept hanging around!

Dad's Pickleball Jokes

Here We Go Again!

What do you call it when no one remembers the score in the middle of the game?

 A DILLemma!

Dad's Pickleball Jokes

Dog gone it!

Why couldn't Scout the dog play with the Pickleballs?

 Because they all belonged to a dog named Pickles!

Printed in the USA
CPSIA information can be obtained
at www.ICGtesting.com
JSHW072349261124
74389JS00002B/2